40 Conversations with Your Soul

A guided journey into self-love

Mary M. Bauer

ISBN 978-0-9990475-3-8

Cover art: chyworks/Shutterstock.com
Author photograph: Shoe Button Photography by Jessica Gilliland
Cover design and page layout: coversbykaren.com

For you sparkly creators who listen to your hearts.

For you kindhearted creators who are pure love in a world that needs it.

For you wise creators who know your truth.

For you compassionate creators who want to embody your highest and best good.

For you, Beautiful, with love…

Also by Mary M. Bauer:

Guarding Clare: A Ransom Mayes Novel

40 Conversations with Your Soul

A guided journey into self-love

Introduction

Hello Beautiful,

And welcome! I'm excited for you. You're about to enter into a collaborative conversation with your loving, wise inner guide who always believes in you, supports your every thought and feeling without judgment, and is in your corner 24/7 helping you create your desires and experiences without question.

This is exactly why I journal every day. I need this intimate connection with the wisest part of me that sees a *way* bigger picture, and knows how to love me through my toughest challenges and saddest times. My Soul teaches me how to embrace and use my creative powers so my life feels enjoyable and peaceful, like something I get to do rather than something I have to struggle through.

But it wasn't always this way for me. Before I started journaling, I was angry. A lot. And depressed. A lot. When I wasn't working, I was either sleeping or obsessively cleaning everything—my home, my car, the garage, the kids, the yard. I couldn't put my finger on it, but it seemed like there should be more. You know? *More.*

From a young age I saw white light around every-thing—trees, plants, animals, people, buildings, furniture. Everything. And I knew things ahead of time, like if I was in danger and how to avoid it. I was the kid everyone told their problems to, and then they felt better. I also had this nagging, relentless feeling that there was something I was supposed to do.

My friends and family never seemed to have these thoughts or experiences. I'd get blank stares or teased if I talked about it, so I quit talking about it. And I quit seeing white light and knowing things. They were replaced with righteous anger, anxiety, depression, and feelings of unwor-thiness. I lost touch with my authentic nature—the soul of who I really was, and no longer remembered the person I was born to be. I let the world tell me who I was, and for a while I believed it. I had a nice home, a handsome, hard-working husband, two beautiful wise children, lots of friends, a career I liked, a rich church life. I should've been happy, so why wasn't I? What was wrong with me? It seemed like I was forever searching. For what, I didn't know.

And I had questions. Lots of them. Big ones, little ones, angry ones, stuff about the nature of the universe, and the nature of God. I wanted to know the reason for the injustices I saw in the world, and the devasting illnesses that robbed people of their loved ones.

I was a nurse at the time and witnessed a lot of fear and regret around death. One man in particular I can't forget. He died screaming, his eyes filled with terror in spite of the love surrounding him, and I wanted to know why. There seemed no end to the suffering, and I felt much of it as though it were mine. I'd walk into a party, or a bar, or work, or anywhere, and automatically know which person was in pain and needed help.

And I knew I needed help, too. I had questions no one could answer and it was driving me crazy. Until one day I picked up a notebook and out of angry frustration scribbled a question: *What's the purpose of life?*

Surprisingly, an answer immediately popped into my head without my thinking: *Life is for you.*

Life is for me? I wrote.

Yes. The good and the bad of it. The up and the down of it. All of it. All for you so you can create and experience whatever you dream—the darkest shadows, or the brightest light. You are not limited in any way. The power that builds universes courses through your veins. You've forgotten the great power that hears and fulfills your every command through your thoughts and feelings. You are not a victim of circumstance. You are the creator of your circumstance, as is everyone on the planet. What do you wish to create now?

This two-sided, back and forth conversation with my Soul Self began in 1994 and continues daily. I've filled several large totes with these notebooks of wisdom, encouragement, and answers to my questions. And man, did it help.

I feel different now, calm, relaxed, excited about my life, and more in alignment with my natural self. I no longer force myself to do something I don't want to, or stress myself out trying to make something happen. Instead, I listen to my inner guidance and take action on what feels like fun. I see the purposeful perfection to everything in my life—even some things that before I would've thought of as bad.

That's powerful, because while my outer circumstance isn't always immediately changeable, my inner world can be with the changing of my thought. Change my thought, which is the creative energy blueprint for the experience, and my perception of the experience automatically changes, too.

This is how I use my beautiful connection to my Soul Self—as a way to examine and change my perceptions so I can see the bigger 360 picture that my Soul sees. This brings me into conscious alignment with Source Energy which is eternally creating whatever I'm thinking and feeling without limitation or opinion.

I've come to realize that life really is for me. And life is for you too, Beautiful. That's what this whole book is about—a way to connect and receive your best advice from your wisest and most loving counselor. This book can help you understand how to create the life you want.

As you read through the conversations, imagine it *is* your Soul talking, offering its gentle guidance and encouragement to view yourself as your Soul does—a brave, wise, loving being doing the best you can. There's real power in allowing your Soul to embrace you and reveal your innermost truth as you sort through your thoughts and feelings by using the conversation questions.

Do your best to answer the questions. Don't rush if something doesn't come to you right away. Let it be okay to just sit with the question, or ask a new one. Set the intention that it's possible for you to know all answers for your highest good. Rub your skin lightly back and forth while you ask. This activates cellular memory buried in your nervous system. It knows everything about you. As you rub your skin, ask, "If I *could* know, what would the answer be?" A quiet thought or image might pop into your mind. Don't judge what comes. Keep going. Dig deeper. Ask more questions until you're satisfied.

Use this book in whatever way feels natural to you in the moment—jot notes, journal, doodle, draw. Start at the beginning and do one conversation a day, or once a week, or skip around to the conversation that feels right. You'll know.

This is your sacred Soul conversation, Beautiful. It has the potential to bring your answers and shift your perception into an understanding of your immense power, how you create your experiences, and how to fully step into a life you love.

Conversation 1

Beautiful,

You are unique. Do you know what that means? Do you know how many stars collided, how many planets formed, how many cells divided, how many decisions were made, how many ancestors before you, how many events that had to occur just to make you exactly the way you are?

Your light, your wisdom, your exquisite beauty is beyond compare. Only you can think, feel, see, know, taste, hear, sense, and understand the world in your specific way. You are the essence of God experiencing God. What you think stirs great creative energy into form.

So, what are you thinking, Beautiful? How are you expressing your uniqueness? Are you comparing your life to someone else's? This is a waste of your powerful creative energy, because there's no one with whom you can compare. There isn't any more of you. And isn't that wonderful? Isn't that perfect? Would you enjoy shopping at a store that had 8 billion of one thing? How boring would that be?

Nature understands its uniqueness. When a flower emerges from the bud, unfurling its brilliant glory, it's not measuring itself against any other flower or pressuring itself to be like its neighbor. The flower expresses its inherent beauty, already carried within its roots, in a complete and natural way, not wanting anything more—not wanting anything less.

You are so much more than a flower. You are Source Energy expressing its evolutionary consciousness through experience. Embrace your uniqueness by fully exploring and expressing every thought and feeling that feels good and right to you. Claim your birthright as only you can. Be you.

Is there something you're burning to share, do, try, or be? Write it down, and read it out loud. This brings focus to your desires helping turn your unique thoughts and feelings into the experiences you most want.

My journey today

My journey today

Conversation 2

Beautiful,

There are times this world can shatter you—a death, an illness, money loss, job loss, home loss, a family member in trouble. It can seem too much to bear. And it is, Beautiful. It is too much to bear—alone. This is the most important time to remember where your strength comes from, where your courage comes from, where the essence of your Being is rooted.

The power that formed Universes is within you. There's nothing you're not an integral part of. Your family is everywhere. Reach out and let someone tend to your heart when it's broken. Let your healing begin within the embrace of another. It's an act of great bravery to ask for what you need.

What is it you need, Beautiful? How has this world shattered you? Can you tell someone? If you can't, please tell your God essence—the Source of All—everything that's in your heart. Write it out, or talk it out, or shout it out. Just get it out. Breathe. You'll feel better and more peaceful when your body is free of the bottled-up emotions.

Children are brilliant in the way they release a strong feeling. They jump, or dance, or pitch a fit, or scream. And they do it immediately as the emotion arises. They instinctively know they'll feel better, because their body isn't holding an intense vibration that's not aligned with their natural feelings of joy and ease.

Release your emotions in the way that feels helpful to you. Do it right away and as often as you need to.

My journey today

My journey today

Conversation 3

Beautiful,

We are creating a shiny new world together. It's a world that celebrates uniqueness, encourages all opinions, isn't afraid to express authenticity without backlash, can look one another in the eyes and see the Self reflecting, and has had enough of destructive thought patterns and behaviors.

In this world we're creating, we listen with reverent respect to one another knowing this is what we want, too. Our inclusiveness is our demonstration that we understand we belong to each other—we're all created from the same God DNA that powers the sun that lights our world. We are Love reflecting Love in our unique way, and we know it.

Beautiful, it takes so little of your immense energy to create a world you wish to live in. Examine your thoughts. Are they focused on unity, peace, good will, and joy for yourself?

What are your thoughts? What do you spend most of your time thinking about? If you knew all your thoughts created the life you have, would you continue to think the same things?

Use your powerful thoughts to create what you most want in life. Use phrases like: I am strong. I am wise. I know how to use my wisdom to create what I want. I trust my inner guidance and act on the ideas I feel enthusiastic about. I am focused. I know how to focus for my highest and best good. I know everything's working out for me. I can feel my life improving. I have unlimited access to my highest Source power.

Think of more phrases that feel good to you and write them down. Begin with words like I am, I have, I know, I trust, I can. Focus on the feeling you get as you write down your phrases and say them out loud. Feel yourself getting lighter and more energized as you think of more phrases.

Get excited! You're working with enormous creative power. Your focused thoughts and feelings direct Source Energy to bring your good. Do this consistently for 30 days and you'll see evidence of the shiny new world you're creating.

My journey today

My journey today

Conversation 4

Beautiful,

I'm in love with you. Your essence sparkles with compassion, hope for the future, and the wholeness of a heart healed by inner wisdom and joy. At times, yours has been a path of deep sorrow and pain, a confusion about the fork in the road and which way to go. Which way leads to freedom, to light?

Beautiful, you are the courageous one who has ventured onto the rockier path and blazed the trail for others. Your courage has led to the deep knowing that it's all light, it's all love, and now you shine the beacon from the other side.

When you're in despair, Beautiful, faced with challenges that make your heart ache, think of those times when you've felt this way before and got through it. Not only got through it, but thrived. How did you find your way out of the pain? Did you confide in a friend? Then do so again, right now. Don't wait another minute to relieve yourself of this great burden. Did you exercise or journal? Then do that, too. Perhaps you found solace in nature, or church, or in a book. Do all those things and more.

Take baths, deep breathe, join a club, learn something new. Do whatever it takes to feel supported, nurtured, and loved. Be super easy on yourself, and trust your process. Rest in the knowledge you've gotten through this before, and keep your thoughts firmly on the belief that the best possible outcome is already on its way. Your Soul, who loves you completely and sees your bigger picture, knows this is true even if it doesn't feel like it in the moment.

When have you been in despair before and gained valuable wisdom from it? What was the wisdom? How can you best nurture and love yourself today?

My journey today

My journey today

Conversation 5

Beautiful,

Everything is energy. Energy creates everything. You are energy. You didn't create energy, but your thoughts direct this limitless, powerful force and mold it into what you see in your daily life. Imagine that, Beautiful. Your thoughts tell Source Energy exactly what to create. In essence, you purchase everything you see in your life with your thoughts. Your thoughts are your power of purchase.

Examine your thoughts. Are they filled with what you don't want? Because those thoughts have the same purchasing power. Instead, direct Source Energy by telling it what you *do* want. Use powerful statements like:

- Opportunities for my greatest good come to me easily and freely.

- My life unfolds with grace and ease in the best way possible for me.

- I act on the ideas that feel good to me.

- I know Life is always working for me and bringing my highest good.

- I allow my good to come to me in the fastest, best way possible.

Write down as many statements as you can think of that put you directly in the flow of your Source Energy.

My journey today

My journey today

Conversation 6

Beautiful,

Like your fingerprint, you have your own unique energy vibration. You can pull on gloves to hide your fingerprint, and you can move into your emotions to change your vibration.

When you're sad or depressed, you feel down and have a difficult time motivating yourself—like you have no energy at all. But when you're excited about something, it feels like you're soaring with energy. Emotions change the vibration of your energy.

Here's a couple easy techniques to stay balanced in your energy field. They can help build your vibration when you're feeling unsettled.

Technique 1:

- Relax and get comfy. Close your eyes. Visualize all of your energy coming back as you inhale deeply through your nose.

- Exhale a short, powerful burst out through your mouth, and as you do, visualize any energy you're holding that isn't yours or no longer serves you, re-leased back to the Universe as sparkling bright light. (Trust that the Universe knows exactly what to do with this energy.)

- Repeat three times. Your shoulders will feel much lighter—like a weight has been lifted.

Technique 2:

- Close your eyes, take a deep breath, and say your name out loud three times.

- As you do this technique, pay attention to your heart area. You'll feel a subtle movement or click during one of the times you call your name. (You might feel a movement through your shoulder or neck instead of your heart.)

- When you say your name, you're consciously calling back your energy. If you don't feel anything, call your name three times again. Try using your full birth name, or your married name, or whatever name you resonate with most. The movement is subtle, but after this exercise you'll feel more like yourself again.

What did you notice after doing these techniques? Do you feel better? Can you notice a difference?

My journey today

My journey today

Conversation 7

Beautiful,

Your body is a miraculous sensing device that operates automatically through the Subconscious Mind. From the more than 3,000 touch receptors on each fingertip, to the 40 trillion cells that create every system, there's no doubt about it—your mind/body is super intelligent.

However, the mind/body is not the thinker of you. It's the doer. It diligently and steadfastly constructs everything using the vibrational thought and emotion blueprints you send it, and it doesn't judge or contradict those blueprints. It says, "Yes, boss. Right away, boss." To everything. It won't talk back. It takes no time off. It just constructs whatever you dream up in a perfectly flawless manner.

And you can prove it. How many times have people around you been sick, but not you? You didn't have time to get sick, and that's the thought blueprint your subconscious used to keep you healthy.

Your beautiful Subconscious Mind listens and obeys all your thoughts and emotions. It hears and creates from every story you tell yourself. These stories are huge influencers. Tell the story often enough with increased feeling, and it becomes your belief. And what you know to be true, shows up in your life as evidence. It doesn't matter if you don't like the experience you're having. Subconscious Mind is a doer and creates whatever you believe without judgement.

So how do you know what kind of storyteller you are? You'll know by how you feel and what you see in your life. This is wonderful news, because you can always change your mind and think something different. Start by becoming aware of what you're now telling yourself and if it's negative, stop telling that story. Focus on what you want and start creating those new blueprints.

Use your amazing imagination to immerse yourself in the world of your dreams. What are you doing? Who's with you? Where are you living? What is it you want? How did you get it? Write down your new story and read it out loud.

My journey today

My journey today

Conversation 8

Beautiful,

Through your thoughts and feelings, you're creating your idea of life in every moment. But are you aware of what you're thinking and feeling? Do you know what you're creating? Are you sabotaging what you want most?

Take stock of your life. This *is* what you've created so far. Your life right now is the result of every thought, every decision, every feeling, every word, every action that you've already taken. Your present moment *is* the created reality of your past thoughts and feelings.

Observe and evaluate your life objectively. Determine what's not serving you and begin again by consciously choosing the thoughts aligned with what you want to see in your life. By thinking about what you want, and letting yourself feel how good it is to have it, you're literally creating your future right now in the present moment. It's almost like laying a solid brick path in front of you, brick by brick (thought by thought) that leads directly to your highest good.

Take action on the thoughts and ideas that inspire you, even if it's something as simple as an inner urge to take a walk. These inner urgings are your Soul talking, putting you in the exact right place at the right time.

Now, think about the prompts you've ignored because they seemed insignificant, or too good to be true. Pay attention to what comes to mind. Notice the quality of the thought. Does it feel expansive and freeing? Maybe a little exciting? Write it down. These are the thoughts to act on.

My journey today

My journey today

Conversation 9

Beautiful,

Have you ever put bread in a toaster, pushed down the lever, and nothing happened? No toast...until you realized the toaster wasn't plugged in. This is pretty much what happens when you're not plugged into your real Source power.

Nothing works when you're distracted by pain, anxiety, blame, guilt, regret. You're basically plugged into a story in your head and not Source Energy. Letting these thoughts run wild without editing, creates the opposite of what you want.

But there's a lot you can do to change this. Here's a couple simple techniques:

- If you catch yourself replaying the same frustrating or depressing thoughts over and over, you can stop the mind chatter by thinking of a predetermined word. Any word you like: angel, pizza, your dog's name, or anything you decide. Once the mind has been redirected by your stop word, you can choose your next thoughts.

- Whenever you notice your mind on automatic sewage dump, congratulate yourself. Celebrate! It's a great moment of awareness. Pat yourself on the back and say, *Good job, you're brilliant!* Then immediately choose your next thoughts that are more aligned with what you want to see in your life. Do this consistently and your brain gets the message to look for your good.

Be gentle with yourself, Beautiful. Breaking a pattern takes practice, but you will succeed. Start by writing down your stop word. Practice saying it a few times.

My journey today

My journey today

Conversation 10

Beautiful,

There's nothing wrong with wanting more in your life. Wanting more is an acknowledgment that you're a powerful creator. You're not meant to be entirely happy with your life as it is. Satisfied, yes, but always eager for more. Life is designed to cause you to want more in order to expand your experience as a creator into your newest and greatest version of self.

So, look around at your world. Is this what you want? Because this is what you've created so far. Is there something in your life right now you'd like to change? Maybe you'd like a more interesting job, or a different home, or a partner who understands you better? But you won't help your situation if you're focused on what you don't want.

For example, if you keep focusing on your jerk boss and how boring your work is, you can expect more of the same. You're literally bringing yourself more opportunities to experience your thoughts. Instead, only think about what you actually want and state it in the present tense, such as: My work is fulfilling. I feel empowered. I work with the most creative, enlightened people.

Take a deep breath and pay attention to how much lighter you feel as you make your declarations. Imagine how good it feels to have exactly what you want.

Stay with this good feeling as long as you're able, then watch how everything shifts in your world. Suddenly the boss becomes nicer or quits, and the new boss is a dream to work with. Or, out of the blue, you're offered your perfect job. Or your perception changes to the point that these things no longer bother you.

Think of a circumstance you'd like to change, focus on what you want and write it down. You don't have to know how or when the circumstance will change, only that you're no longer creating more of it with your thoughts and feelings.

My journey today

My journey today

Conversation 11

Beautiful,

Did you know you are a master creating your universe? Is it possible for you to believe that you brought yourself to this life, to this time period, and surrounded yourself with all the people and circumstances you needed to have the specific experiences you're now having?

Can you trust in your highest wisdom that you intended to have the experiences you're having for a good reason? Can you develop an inquisitiveness that permits self-discovery no matter the circumstance? Is it possible that everything in your life is happening for you?

When you're confused or facing something painful, allow your soul to soothe and comfort you. Ask your soul: What am I up to? What is the purpose of this particular experience? What am I to notice? Why have I created this person to trigger me?

Ask: Am I ready to change my perception about this circumstance and see it as a way to transform a debilitating belief I have about myself? Am I ready to know who I am and how to step into my vast powers as a Conscious Creator? Am I ready to ask for the help I need to transform my life into what I want and deserve?

Am I ready to accept the master within me?

My journey today

My journey today

Conversation 12

Beautiful,

Did you know you have a Soul message center inside your body? You do. It's your heart. Love and joy flow directly through your heart as high vibe inspiration, peace, and well-being.

Take a look at your heart. What kind of shape is it in? Is your inbox so stuffed with stagnant emotions and bitter memories that there's no room for your Source mail? Are you missing out on your most important life-affirming messages?

If so, journaling is a quick way to declutter your heart inbox. Write down everything that comes to your mind. Write all your pain, all your hatreds, all your dreams, all your goals, all your unworthiness, guilt, doubt, fears. Write all your regrets, jealousies, worries, sorrows, traumas. Write as fast as you can without judgement for what comes, and don't read anything. Let everything pour out of you. Your heart knows what needs to be released.

Then burn everything immediately with the intention that all released thoughts and emotions convert to sparkly creative energy.

And that's it. Write. Burn. Write. Burn. Write. Burn. But absolutely NO judging or reading. You may have to empty your heart ten times, or one hundred times, or one thousand times, or more. But the day will come, Beautiful, when your heart feels light and spacious, and full of love and appreciation for everything in your life. That's when you know your heart inbox is open and ready to receive your Source messages.

My journey today

My journey today

Conversation 13

Beautiful,

Has anyone ever criticized you and laughed when you felt hurt by their words? Did they tell you they were only joking?

A backhanded criticism veiled as a joke is sort of like receiving a bouquet of thorny rose stems. Technically roses, but totally not welcome.

If this has happened to you, Beautiful, you need to speak up right away and not internalize the anger and hurt. A joke is something you both enjoy, and the person needs to be called on their words. However, choose your own words with compassion knowing the person has given you an amazing opportunity to get clear on what's true for you and what's not—what you'll tolerate, and what you won't.

Remember, what you think and feel, you create. So gentle with your tongue, Beautiful, or you're just passing around the same thorns.

If you're holding a grudge or resentment toward someone because of their thoughtlessness, write down everything about the circumstance you now see as a benefit. Maybe this was the catalyst that got you to speak up for yourself? Or maybe you ended a toxic relationship because you realized your worth?

Try to find five benefits to the circumstance. Once you understand what you've gained, the hurting ends.

My journey today

My journey today

Conversation 14

Beautiful,

How good are you at accepting compliments? If someone tells you that you're beautiful, do you automatically begin listing your faults? "Beautiful? Me?" you say, "I have the worst hair and need to lose 10 pounds. But thanks, anyway."

Your Soul only sees you as you are—gorgeous, wise, loving. But you won't experience yourself as beautiful if you can't fathom it no matter how many times you're told. Nothing exists for you that your mind can't accept as real.

But the mind can be trained. Start by looking for one thing about your body you can fully appreciate—like your feet. Aren't your feet great? You wouldn't be able to walk without them. And don't you love your tongue? Without your tongue, how would you swallow? And what about your strong neck? You wouldn't be able to lift your head without it.

List all the things about your body you'd miss if you didn't have them, and appreciate what they do for you. By appreciating your body in a conscious, deliberate way, you're reprograming your brain to look for the good.

This works for all compliments, whether it's about a talent you refuse to acknowledge, the home you live in, your family, everything. Retrain your brain to be on the hunt for your good with everything in your life, and you'll experience more of it.

My journey today

My journey today

Conversation 15

Beautiful,

Your gifts are many, not the least is your body. Embedded within your skin are millions of sensing receptors. The receptors take information from your environment and send it as a signal to your nervous system, which in turn sends signals to the spinal column and brain, triggering action. In each fingertip alone you have more than three thousand receptors. Three thousand! Without them you wouldn't know hot from cold, how much pressure it takes to choose a ripe tomato, or the difference between sandpaper and the velvet skin of a newborn child.

Your body also has a built-in stress reliever. When you're feeling overwhelmed with emotion, tears are your body's natural release and detoxifier. Crying is the way your body transforms an intense emotion into peaceful calm. Don't try to stop this natural process, let your tears come. You'll feel better.

It's also easy to tune into your body to find out what it wants. Maybe you're getting the feeling to go for a walk, or to get up and stretch, or get more sleep. Your body sends you signals about the nutrients it needs. Sometimes you'll get muscle cramps if you're low on calcium, potassium, magnesium, or water. Sometimes you'll have food cravings. As you choose your food, pay attention to your body's subtle clues. When you're in a restaurant, touch the choices on the menu and as you go down the list, how does your body react--queasy, bland, belching, excitement, mouthwatering? Beautiful, do you trust your perfect body intelligence by acting on the signals it sends to keep it healthy, vibrant, and strong? What is one message from your body you can act on today?

My journey today

My journey today

Beautiful,

Begin each day with three deep breaths—in through the nose, exhale long through the mouth. Say to yourself: Love, light, and healing energy flows through me for my highest good. Take one more deep breath, and then get on with your day in whatever manner is best for you.

This simple, yet powerful technique has lasting benefits. The deep breaths bring more oxygen into your beautiful body creating stress-reducing endorphins that boost your immune system. The affirmative statement helps your brain let go of old patterns that are no longer beneficial, and intentionally connects you with Source Energy where all things are possible.

What other things can you do to lessen your stress, bring more appreciation for your body, and connect with Source Energy—your God Essence? How can you be easier on yourself and show yourself more love?

My journey today

My journey today

Conversation 17

Beautiful,

You may not yet know it, but within you is the power of more than a thousand suns. You are not small by any means, nor are you a victim, a survivor, or any label at all.

It's time to claim your birthright. Know that within your being you hold the ancient wisdom of the mountain, the roaring voice of the lion, the mighty strength and endurance of the ant, the healing of the cleansing flame, the shape-shifting ability of the wind, and the ever-present life within the tree root buried in the darkness.

You, Beautiful, are the dream beyond the stars in human form. You're connected to everything. You're powerful, and brilliant, and loving. Claim your naturalness. Claim your abilities. The world needs you. You need you.

What one thing can you do every day to claim your naturalness?

My journey today

My journey today

Conversation 18

Beautiful,

In my visions of lifetimes past, I've seen you tied and flogged, made to feel wrong for your authentic nature. I've also seen a growing fierceness in you that remembers your powerful birthright to live as you were created, in love and freedom.

I watched you slash through the bindings crafted from someone else's belief, and courageously start anew. I witnessed your grace and beauty as you stood naked beneath roaring waters of sparkling light. And as you step forward, you're forever clothed in these powerful, healing waters. You, Beautiful, wear the waterfall of Love.

Dreams and visions come to jog a forgotten memory that might help or comfort, or perhaps bring clarification of a decision that's been made or needs to be made. Dreams can root up trauma buried in the psyche that's essential for transformation, or give encouragement for a life-changing contemplation.

What visions or dreams have you had lately? What are they telling you?

My journey today

My journey today

Conversation 19

Beautiful,

There's enormous transformational power in your anguished cries and the guttural moans that sear your heart and chill your bones. Don't try to stop them. Let them come. These primitive sounds give voice to what you haven't said and dared not say for eons. These sounds wait, held deep in your memory, until the Soul is ready to unravel every raw, painful untruth ever told or believed about who you are.

When that day comes, Beautiful, go willingly into this sorrowful place that is somehow familiar, yet strangely unknown, and there you'll find all your broken pieces, all your unloved thoughts, all your fearful shadows.

Let them come to you and give them a voice. Let them tell you who they are. They beg for your love. Give them everything they ask for. They are like frightened children, now safe in your arms.

Is there something about yourself you're afraid of? Something you believe is too awful or unforgiveable, and no one will love you if they know this about you? Let this shadow come, Beautiful, and love it completely knowing you made the only choice you could've given your aware-ness in that moment. But you're not that same person. Your choices are different, now. You've had more experiences and have a wider perspective. You're not who you were a year ago, or even twenty minutes ago. You are brand new every second of every day, and you get to decide who that is.

Love the child you were, and write the story of who you are now.

My journey today

My journey today

Conversation 20

Beautiful,

You didn't come to this life without dreams and a way to achieve them. But sometimes when your dreams get buried in pain and life distractions, they can seem like they don't exist.

Beautiful, this is the time to ask, what breaks my heart? Where did I leave my passion? What stirs so deeply inside me that I can't live without it?

And then listen. Be still. Your heart knows the way to your dreams. Write down everything that comes to your mind, whether it makes sense to you now or not. Visualize what you wish to see in your life. What feels good to you? What feels joyful? What interests you? What would you like to know more about? What feels like something you get to do?

Write down these thoughts and know you have what it takes to bring your dreams to life. Be fearless and take the steps you're led to take. Source Energy is listening. What are you telling It to create with you?

My journey today

My journey today

Conversation 21

Beautiful,

What lights you up? What do you do just for you? Where do you turn for balance in your life? Where do you find joy? Where do you find peace? What does fulfillment mean to you? Are you fulfilled? When you wake, how do you feel? How do you feel as you go to sleep?

These are important questions, and you're answering them 24/7 with every one of your thoughts. Beautiful, know your answers, think of nothing else, and let nothing stop you from becoming your most expansive conscious self.

My journey today

My journey today

Conversation 22

Beautiful,

Your thoughts are powerful. A continuous thought creates your belief. Your belief becomes knowing. What you know becomes your truth. Your experience will bring evidence of what you know. Your experience will cause thoughts, which create the loop all over again. You are always in the process of creating your idea of reality. So, what are you thinking, Beautiful? What do you believe?

What do you believe about your body? That it's highly intelligent and knows exactly what to do to heal itself, and will do so with loving thoughts?

What do you believe about yourself? Do you believe you're a Source creator with the power to change your reality just by changing your thoughts?

What do you believe about other people? That they are Source creators in unique form with their own version of reality?

What do you believe about the world? Do you believe that you're related to everything? That nothing is separate from you because it's all Source/God experiencing Source/God in limitless forms?

What do you believe about your future? That you are the Conscious Creator of what you wish to see in your life, and your thoughts stir great Source Energy into action?

What do you believe, Beautiful? And where did these beliefs come from? Are they truly yours based on your experience? Or do they belong to someone else? Do your beliefs still serve you? Do they fill you with joy, peace, enthusiasm?

You see what you believe you see. Are you ready to see something else? Are you ready to believe something else? What is the grandest version of yourself you're ready to believe? These are important questions. They create your reality. Take all the time you need to answer them.

My journey today

My journey today

Conversation 23

Beautiful,

There are times when you have no control over what happens in life—the death of a loved one, a debilitating illness, an estranged relationship, or loss of any kind. You're grief-stricken, and heartbroken, and every fiber of your being feels raw. Nothing makes sense. You know you're not the same person, and there's no going back.

But, Beautiful, grief has a purpose. It expands your world like nothing else can. With grief comes new emotions you can't quite name, but they're there and you feel their power. They crash over you like heavy waves, and fill your gut and your bones and your throat with strangled anguish, only to be carried away by the stunning stillness of a sunset, and in this moment everything stops. In this moment there's depth and richness you hadn't noticed before. And you start to think maybe, just maybe, there's more. You begin to appreciate things differently—a kind word, a friendly smile, a gentle touch. Everything seems amplified and goes straight to the heart.

Beautiful, when grief comes to you, embrace it. Explore its vast open chambers, and its hidden nooks and crannies. Look at all of it as a help to you, a place to empty your sorrow, your confusion, your bitterness, and anger. Think of how a rainbow transforms a stormy sky into a magical wonder. Pour your pain-filled heart into grief, and let it transform your sorrow into an even deeper love.

What bitterness does your heart hold that you can now give to grief? Let the great transformer wash away your sorrow and fill you with peace.

My journey today

My journey today

Conversation 24

Beautiful,

How can I impress upon you the scope of your magnificence and power? There's nothing small or weak about you. You create everything in your life as a way to experience who you are, and what it means to you.

This is a huge undertaking, Beautiful—to fully know and understand your world as you've created it. If you're experiencing resistance, blame, or judgement about yourself or someone else, know you've created these situations and people to trigger you. They will show you every thought and feeling inside that needs your understanding and tender loving care.

If you're feeling anything other than love, know for certain it's yours to look at because you feel it. This part of you knows it belongs to you, and wonders why you think it's so terrible and shouldn't be there? It was created through your thoughts and feelings, which move Source Energy into action. The pain comes from rejection of your own creation.

Take deep breaths, Beautiful, and embrace these painful thoughts and feelings with love. When you were a child, you made the decisions of a child. Not wrong, just not aware of a larger perspective. You're different now. Your awareness has expanded, and your choices, too. Simply love your past creations, knowing you did the best you could, then make new choices.

Your power lies in loving all you've created. This is how you transform all pain. What one painful thought can you love today. Write it down.

My journey today

My journey today

Conversation 25

Beautiful,

How do you know if something is right for you? This can be a tough question, but you have tools to help you figure it out.

When making a decision, pay attention to how you feel. Does it feel like something you *get to* do, or something you *should* do? Do you feel resistance, uneasiness, or queasiness in your body? Or do you feel light, excited, peaceful?

When something is right for you, you won't have to talk yourself into it. You'll want to do it. Trust these signals. They're giving you valuable information about your highest path.

If you ignore your intuition and end up having a challenging experience, try not to feel guilty for it, or have any regrets. Instead, tell yourself that now you know exactly what it feels like when you go against your inner guidance, and it'll be easier next time because of the experience.

Now, think of a time when you went against your intuition. How did that feel? Think of another time when you followed your intuition. How did that feel? Is there a difference between the two feelings? How does your guidance show up for you when you need to make a decision?

My journey today

My journey today

Beautiful,

There will be times when you feel deep disappointment—you're passed over for a promotion, an illness returns, a friend breaks a confidence, a family member screws up, an old habit reappears. Even when you achieve exactly what you want, disappointment can surface. But don't be deceived. Disappointment can be a distractor if you're not aware of its purpose.

If you're feeling disappointed, it's an indication that there's something you don't yet know about yourself, and it invites you to take a closer look.

Be gentle with yourself and ask deep questions: Where does this feeling come from? Have I sacrificed my inner peace for something I can't control? Have I gotten lost in a story and stuck in a mind loop that replays over and over? Have I forgotten that my thoughts and feelings are creative? What is disappointment telling me? What have I given my power to?

Beautiful, when disappointment knocks, open your heart wide. Greet this friend with grace and compassion for the powerful reminders it brings. End your mind loop by using your stop word, and congratulate yourself for your expanded awareness.

What do you choose to think about, now?

My journey today

My journey today

Conversation 27

Beautiful,

Is there something from your past you can't let go? Something you're still beating yourself up over? Would you choose something different, now? If so, understand it's because you are different now. You've had more experiences, and it's those experiences that allow an expanded awareness. You see things from a wider perspective.

Compassion for self is the ability to see that you always make the right decision based on your awareness. Don't make yourself wrong for a past decision when it was the only choice you could've made at the time. Accept that you did the best you could do, and begin fresh by consciously deciding what you want, now.

Source Energy is limitless creative power without an "off" button. It says YES to everything you think and feel without judgment or preference. When you think about your past and feel the emotion, you're using Source Energy to create more of the same. Do you want more of the same? Is there something more to be gained by bringing your past into your future?

Only you know the answer. You're absolutely free to think and feel in whatever way suits you, but claim your creative power by developing an awareness for how you build your future.

What do you want to see in your life, Beautiful, and is that what you're thinking?

My journey today

My journey today

Conversation 28

Beautiful,

Here's a fun fact about Source Energy/God Essence— every reality exists, and you're creating your version as a perception in your mind. Nothing exists for you that's not in your mind.

Another fun fact—you can change your mind.

What reality are you creating with your thoughts, feelings, words, and actions? Are these thoughts, feelings, words, and actions in alignment with what you wish to create? If not, what do you need to change? If they are in alignment, can you expand your vision into your dream reality? How would you do that? What thoughts, feelings, words, actions do you need to drop, or add, to create your ultimate life?

- Write down what you want, and be specific. Do this daily, when you first wake before the thinking starts. This creates a new brain pattern.

- As you write, feel what it'd be like to have what you want. See yourself in this future. Feel the certainty that this thing is yours or you wouldn't have wanted it.

- Ask your Highest Intuitive Self for your first step to bring you dream to reality. Write that down, too.

- Schedule time on your calendar to take action on the steps needed to make your dream real. Focus solely on your heart's desire, and no beating yourself up for what you don't yet see. It's coming.

- Get an accountability partner. Check in with them once a week to keep you on track.

My journey today

My journey today

Conversation 29

Beautiful,

It's hard to be the master of your thoughts when you feel worried, stressed, or exhausted. Here's a powerful technique to support your nervous system, reduce anxiety, and create connection within your body by sending energy up your spine. This simple procedure is perfect for strengthening your energy field so you feel more like yourself.

Start by placing your middle finger on your belly button, and the middle finger from your other hand on your brow chakra (center of the forehead). Then simply push in at both spots, and pull up.

As you do this technique, close your eyes and breathe slowly and deeply, in through your nose, out through your mouth six times, or until you feel better.

And that's it. You might experience some tingling in your body, or a sense of lightness and relief. Everyone is different, and you'll feel what's right for you.

What other things can you do to help yourself recharge and rejuvenate when you know your energy is low? Make a list so you have some options ready when you need them.

My journey today

My journey today

Conversation 30

Beautiful,

Do you make decisions according to how you feel? Or do you rely on your intuition when making decisions? There is a difference.

Decisions based on how you feel might not be accurate. That's because feelings are interwoven with experiences, which create your perception of reality. As an example: you look down a dark alley and get a creepy feeling. Because of your feeling, you decide not to walk down the alley.

The creepy feeling could've come from watching a scary movie of a dark, isolated place where something bad happened. That impression is stored in your brain as emotional memory. The dark alley will trigger the memory and you'll make your decision because of the feeling, which isn't based on a real experience.

This is true of all kinds of situations. Maybe you hate dogs because, as a child, you unconsciously picked up on a parent's fear of them. The fear you have about dogs wasn't even yours to begin with, but it will feel like yours. You may discover you like dogs, but the fearful emotion will stop you from having an authentic experience. You're stuck in a perception based on a feeling.

You've had many experiences that produce your feelings, which create your perception of life. Intuition, however, doesn't usually come with a feeling. It's more neutral, and quiet, and there's no great way to explain it other than it's an absolute knowing within you.

When you base a decision on your intuition, there's no fear, or anxiety, or second-guessing. You're certain, and you don't feel the need to defend or convince anyone of your decision.

Intuition is your highest Source connection. There's a joyful ease to life the more often you follow your intuition. What have you noticed about your intuition? How is it different from your feelings?

My journey today

My journey today

Conversation 31

Beautiful,

So much in this world is belief masquerading as fact. Belief is not the same thing as fact. Remember, at one time people believed the earth was flat.

Be the explorer of your own truth. Be the scientist who says, what if everything I know about this particular situation is false? Start over as if you know nothing. Ask yourself, "Is this true for me? How do I feel about that?"

Begin a daily awareness practice by noticing your thoughts and feelings and what they create. What is happening in your life? What is your body experiencing? How does this relate to what you're thinking? If you determine something is not for you, do you honor your intuition and stop what you're doing, or do you force yourself to continue? How does that feel? Is there resistance in your body? Does it feel like you have to do it, versus you get to?

Your truth is often determined by your beliefs, and not your intuition. If you believe you must work hard for your money, you will create the experience to bring evidence of your truth. But, Beautiful, there are many people who don't work hard at all, and still have lots of money. Think of the songwriter who works for fifteen minutes on a song, and sells it for millions.

What is true for you, Beautiful? How do you know your truth? What is your evidence, and what is it based on?

My journey today

My journey today

Conversation 32

Beautiful,

Adversity can offer the greatest opportunity to go deeper into your true Source strength, where there is peace, calm, well-being, vibrancy, and abundance. But when you're struggling, confused, angry, or when everything is going wrong, it's hard not to go down the rabbit hole and lash out. You want the hurt to go away.

Here's a simple way to raise your energy vibration in order to connect with your Highest Source Self:

- Close your eyes and lift your face to the sun.

- Place your hand over your heart, and take several slow, deep breaths.

- Keep your eyes closed and as you breathe, you'll begin to notice an array of neon colors. Bright colors: red, orange, yellow, green, blue, cobalt blue, purple, gold, white. These are the colors of your energy centers (chakras).

- Breathe in these colors as they appear and you'll start to feel better.

The sun's rays feed your centers with powerful light energy. You'll see the colors you need most, but if you can't see anything, activities like walking help open your energy field. Alternate between walking and facing the sun. Write down your experience. What did you notice as you brought in your colors? How did your body feel? Did you receive insights?

Note: The chakras, their colors, and the energy they embody~

Root (or Base): red—stability, bravery, courage, grounded, strength, determination, security

Sacral: orange—harmony, spontaneity, creativity, passion, physical vitality, sacred sensuality and sexuality

Solar Plexus: yellow—intelligence, confidence, personal power, independence, individuality, flexibility, personality, humor, Divine will

Heart: green—joy, faith, compassion, miracles, magic

High Heart (thymus): pink or aqua—selfless devotion to Universal creation, unconditional love, joy

Throat: sky blue—language, communication, magnetism, truth, honesty

Brow (or Third Eye): cobalt blue—psychic vision, clairvoyance, intuition, crystal clear clarity

Crown: purple or pink—Divine wisdom, Divine connection, ascended mastery, ecstasy, bliss, humbleness, illumination

Transpersonal Point: white or gold—Christ consciousness, connection to God Self

My journey today

My journey today

Conversation 33

Beautiful,

What do you tell yourself upon waking? In your mind is the day full of sunshine or rain? Is your mind replaying old bitter stories and holding space for imagined problems? Or are you focused on what you wish to see in your life?

Remember, the quality of your life is directly created, moment by moment, by the quality of your thoughts. What you think matters = turns into matter (physical form/experience).

Everything created in the physical world first begins in your mind with your ideas, dreams, and heart passion. You constantly use thoughts and feelings in the creation of your life.

How incredible to wake and know you are the creator of your dreams. Train your mind to work for you, not against you. Teach your mind to think only the thoughts of your Soul. Ask yourself: What brings me joy? What interests me? What is it I truly want? What one step can I take right now to create what I wish to see? Write it down.

My journey today

My journey today

Conversation 34

Beautiful,

Are you aware of the love and support Mother Earth showers on you every second of every day?

It's true. When in nature, close your eyes, take a deep breath, and listen to the music of a song bird. Can you feel the bird's elated tune ripple through your body, opening and toning your energy centers? Your entire energy field absorbs the joyful vibrations, and you feel better as a result.

And there's more. Have you noticed how the gentle breeze on a summer's eve does more to soothe your troubled mind than any expensive balm? Don't you find relief from your sorrow when you spend time in a cedar grove? Don't you feel awed excitement when you see the vibrant pink of a flamingo?

Manmade therapies pale in comparison to Mother Earth's expansive, life-affirming offerings. Observe, absorb, and listen to her. Learn from her. Notice how her freshly tilled soil opens space for new beginnings. Pay attention to how the fragrant lilac encourages a deeper breath, filling your body with restorative oxygen. Sense how the beauty inspired by the grace of a deer, brings your troubles to a stop, and peace to your heart.

It's all for you—soaring eagles, soft rains, fluffy kittens, brilliant sunsets, clover fields, juicy peaches, apple blossoms, diamond snowflakes, azure lagoons, playful dolphins, grandfather trees, and the depth and possibilities of the night sky.

Open your heart to the great love of Mother Earth. She knows exactly how to lift your spirit and heal your heart. For an entire week notice all the ways you're supported by nature. Journal your awareness. You'll discover how deeply you're loved.

My journey today

My journey today

Conversation 35

Beautiful,

Are you living your truth, or are you attempting to fulfill someone else's wish list? Are you making decisions based on the lighthearted feeling of I *get to*, or do you push yourself to do something because you believe you *should*?

Examine your life, Beautiful. Are you overwhelmed by the pain of manipulation, the frustration of expectation, and the exhaustion of obligation? Are you saying "yes" to something when you really mean "no"?

Then know you've abandoned your truth in favor of someone else's by sacrificing your alignment with who you are. Remember, only you can think your thoughts, feel your emotions, say your words, take your actions, and live your life. This is true even in the worst circumstances.

But be gentle with yourself. Whatever is happening, trust that there's value in your experience, even if in the moment you can't quite see what it is. Maybe this is the incentive you need to commit to what you know to be right for you?

List 5 things that feel like "I get to…"

List 5 things that feel like "I should…"

Which do you do more often? The things you should do, or the things you get to do? Is there something on the "should" list you can eliminate? Are there two things on that list you can eliminate? What one step can you take today to do more things that feel like you get to?

My journey today

My journey today

Conversation 36

Beautiful,

What fear guards your heart? What voice drowns out the whispers of your soul? Unworthiness? Abandonment? Failure? These fears are personal truths held deep in your mind and based on your experiences. Your personal truths generate the results in life you think you deserve.

Beautiful, what you don't remember is fear is not a Soul truth, and you're in the process of healing everything dishonest to your soul. With a shift in perception, every difficulty, confusion, and fear become opportunities to embrace your soul's truth.

You are wise. You are courageous. You are love without conditions, and your soul knows this. Your soul is interested in creating experiences that reflect its truth. Hidden within every fear is a benefit, if you can face it with the eyes of your soul. When you're challenged, or afraid, or lonely, ask: What am I gaining? How is this experience of value to me?

Feel deep within for your answers. How are you different because of this experience? Is there a way for you to go beyond the hurt and fear, and become aware of the benefit?

Think of one painful experience, and list five ways you've changed for the better because of it.

My journey today

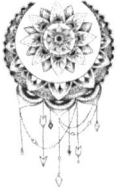

My journey today

Conversation 37

Beautiful,

How quickly you forget your good fortune, and how effortlessly you commit the bad to your memory. No amount of berating, bargaining, or affirmations seems to change what appears a counterproductive behavior. Would it help to know humans are wired this way? The everyday survival of prehistoric ancestors depended on their ability to watch for bad news and fast track it to memory.

But is this how you want to live, Beautiful? Stuck in the Stone Age? You have a choice. It's absolutely possible to train your brain to look for enough safety, satisfaction, connection, fullness, contentment, appreciation, and love.

Begin by consciously looking for little opportunities to experience something good. Experiences are made of information. The brain is like a miraculous computer that sifts through the information and stores it. The nervous system assigns meaning to the information based on your feelings.

To rewire your brain while you're experiencing something good, take a deep breath to slow things down. In that moment become super aware of what you're feeling, and consciously stay with that good experience an extra moment. Feel the good experience within your body. Where do you feel it? How do you sense it? Focus on what is rewarding about it.

By paying attention to the feelings you enjoy a bit longer, you develop new information pathways in the brain. This is how you help the mind/body work for you to break old patterns to create a life you love. Try this exercise throughout the week. Pay attention to how you feel when you're experiencing something good. Feel it in your body for as long as you can. Journal your experience.

My journey today

My journey today

Conversation 38

Beautiful,

Everyone experiences pain. Sometimes it shows up physically as job loss, home loss, an unwanted change in a relationship, an illness, an accident, and more. Pain also shows up emotionally as anxiety, grief, depression, loneliness, and doubt.

When you're in pain, you want to feel better. Everyone does. So, what can you do to improve how you feel?

One thing that's helpful is awareness of what your thoughts and feelings are creating in the collective energy field. This field is an invisible space of pure vibrational energy where everything exits before it becomes physical form and experience.

You telepathically tap into the collective energy field with your mind. And, depending on how you feel, make a withdrawal of energy in the form of a thought.

For example: If you were diagnosed with cancer and are feeling blindsided by it, devastated, vulnerable—will it help to telepathically hear from the collective energy field, *Oh, you poor thing. Cancer. How awful. How scary. So horrible. Cancer is never good...*

Or would you rather hear: I am strong. I am aware. I am loved. I trust my wisdom. I trust my process. I know I've got this. I know my body is super intelligent and knows what to do. I know how to help my body heal. I know my best way. I know what joy is. I am peaceful. I am joyful. I am safe. I have great compassion for myself. I have lots of support.

Put into the collective energy field every thought you most want for yourself. Begin your statements using present tense words like: I am, I have, I trust, I know, I believe, I can, and then finish the sentence with what you want, even if you're thinking of someone else. This is the way you help yourself and others without judging the experience, resisting it, or making it wrong. When the other person taps into the field, the thoughts they'll receive are: I am strong, I am aware, I trust my wisdom…and so on. That way these thoughts are available to anyone who needs them.

Think of some statements you can send to the collective energy field, and write them down.

My journey today

My journey today

Conversation 39

Beautiful,

When you have a great idea, it fills you with excitement and possibilities. Suddenly your world feels clear, light, and expanded. You know you've tapped into a genius beyond your usual thought. This is a heart call, a soul urge, and it wouldn't be in your energy field if it wasn't possible for you to attain. But Beautiful, you must also be the implementer of your dreams, because a great idea without action is worthless.

When the Soul urges you to take action through feelings of excitement, lightness, or curiosity, follow those urges. The same is true for your more subtle promptings—a feeling that you need to be somewhere, or take a specific class, or talk to a certain person. These internal signals may not feel logical, but don't dismiss them. Many times, they provide the next step in the creation of your dreams.

What are your dreams, Beautiful? What deep longing lives in your heart? Have you ever wanted something and got it? How did you get it? Did you follow internal urgings? Did you have an inner knowing that you'd get what you want?

Write out the story of how you got what you wanted as proof of your creative power. Notice the internal messages you got along the way and the steps you were guided to take. Pay attention to all the support you received, and how everything fell into place with ease.

List at least one thing you can do today to follow your guidance.

My journey today

My journey today

Conversation 40

Beautiful,

What you believe to be true, is true for you. But to create exactly what you want you must know how it looks and what it feels like when you get it.

Begin by imagining your perfect day, and imagine BIG—something outrageous! Then, start a journal and date the entry 10 months from today. What are you doing on your outrageously perfect day? Where are you? Who is with you? Are you hiking the Appalachian Trail with your best friend? Are you on vacation with your family at a 5-star European hotel? Maybe it's the first day of your dream job?

Whatever it is, describe every detail of your day in present tense, from the moment you wake, until the second your head hits the pillow. Remember, you're writing about a normal day in your life *after* you already have what you want. For example, if you're hiking the Appalachian Trail, you'll write something like: "This is our 30th day on the trail, and I still pinch myself. I get to wake every morning to a spectacular sunrise, birds singing, and the deep flavor of campfire coffee. There's nothing like it!"

Inject as much feeling and detail into your perfect day as possible. What are you wearing? What are you doing? What do you see? What are you eating? What do you smell and taste? What do you feel? What do you hear? Who are you with, and what are you talking about?

Next, recall at least 5 times in the past (more if you can) when you got exactly what you wanted, and write them down. How did you feel after you got that amazing thing? Why did you want it? How did you know you would get it? What made it materialize? Did you follow a hunch? Did you just *know* you would get it?

Sit with this awareness, immerse yourself in it, until you can sense the excitement you had when you got exactly your heart's desire. Take a couple deep breaths and let this expansive energy vibrate through your whole being. This creative energy is real, and you have a list proving you can manifest whatever you want.

Now, while in this expansive energy, read aloud what you wrote about your perfect day. Expand that good vibe feeling, anchoring it into your body as you read your journal. Your mind doesn't know the difference between what you have now, and what you hold true for you. It wants to close all gaps and align to your truth. You get to say what that is, and Source Energy begins the creation process.

Rewrite or make any changes to your journal as you need to. Go deeper, get more details. Let any thoughts or feelings float away that are not in alignment with your outrageously perfect day. Stay focused on how it feels to have exactly what you want.

Read your journal every day. Take the action steps your intuition prompts you to take. This is how you consciously create your best life using your Source power.

My journey today

My journey today

Beautiful,

This is a great day of celebration. I'm so proud of you. You cracked your own creation code! You know your power and how to use it. You understand that your thoughts and feelings create the perception of your reality. You know if you change your thoughts, a new view of the world opens for you to experience.

You know there's no one to blame for the way you think your thoughts, feel your emotions, say your words, or take your actions. You know you're not a victim or a survivor. You're a creator and you're always creating.

You also know you're not alone. God Source Energy is always with you. It is you. It says YES to every one of your thoughts, every single time. It's a little like the electricity in your home—always present and waiting for you to decide how to use it. Your job is to know your thoughts and stay focused on what you want to create. Take action on the promptings that feel light and exciting to you.

Always remember, you came from the stars and those spaces in-between. You are wisdom, love, beauty, grace, and joy in human form. You are the bravest of the brave. You are beautiful. Your thoughts are powerful. Intend for yourself a magical life.

Beautiful,

Thank you for reading *40 Conversations with your Soul~A guided journey into self-love*. If you enjoyed this book, please consider leaving a rating and review. Your comments really help new books get noticed, and I greatly appreciate every review.

If you'd like to stay in touch, I'd love to hear from you! My contact information is below.

With great love for your journey,
Mary

———————

Email: marymbauer.author@gmail.com
Facebook: https://www.facebook.com/marymbauer.author/
Website: www.marymbauer.com
Weekly newsletter with energy tips and techniques:
https://www.marymbauer.com/insider-optin

About the author

Mary M. Bauer is an energy intuitive, author, listener, laugher, hugger, and longtime journaler. Certified in Healing Touch, ThetaHealing, and Reiki, Mary works within your energy field to help you understand your thoughts and feelings so you can create your best life.

For more information about her books, events, and work, visit www.marymbauer.com

Coloring fun

www.ingramcontent.com/pod-product-compliance
Lightning Source LLC
Chambersburg PA
CBHW071807090426
42737CB00012B/1989